Henry Ward Beecher

The overture of angels

Henry Ward Beecher

The overture of angels

ISBN/EAN: 9783742859037

Manufactured in Europe, USA, Canada, Australia, Japa

Cover: Foto ©ninafisch / pixelio.de

Manufactured and distributed by brebook publishing software
(www.brebook.com)

Henry Ward Beecher

The overture of angels

The Overture of Angels

THE

Overture of Angels

BY

HENRY WARD BEECHER

NEW YORK
J. B. FORD AND COMPANY
1870

Entered according to Act of Congress, in the year 1869, by

J. B. FORD & CO.,

in the Clerk's Office of the District Court for the Southern District of New York.

UNIVERSITY PRESS: WELCH, BIGELOW, & CO.,
CAMBRIDGE.

Publishers' Advertisement.

T HIS little book is issued with a double intent. Complete in itself, it comes to the public most appropriately as a Christmas offering. And yet it bears reference to other topics and broader views than those of which it treats, and gives evidence of being, as it is, a fragment from a larger work. It is that portion of Mr. Beecher's "Life of Jesus, the Christ," which depicts the scenes and events clustering about the birth of our Lord. And the Publishers not only hope that it will be accepted as peculiarly harmonious with the happy Advent season, but believe that the mode in which it presents the record of those holy and precious scenes will arouse a still deeper interest in the forthcoming volume.

THE OVERTURE OF ANGELS

HAD it been the design of Divine Providence that the Gospels should be wrought up like a poem for literary and artistic effect, surely the narrative of the angelic appearances would have glowed in all the colors of an Oriental morning. They are, indeed, to those who have an eye to discern, a wonderful and exquisitely tinted prelude to the dawn of a glorious day. It is not to be supposed that the earth and its dull inhabitants knew what was approaching. But heavenly spirits knew it. There was movement and holy ecstasy in the Upper Air, and angels seem, as birds when new-come in spring, to have flown hither and thither, in songful mood, dipping their white wings into our atmosphere, just touching the earth or glancing along its surface, as sea-birds skim the surface of the sea. And yet birds are far too rude, and wings too burdensome, to express adequately that feeling of unlabored angelic motion which the narrative produces upon the imagination. Their airy and gentle coming would perhaps be better compared to the glow of colors flung by the sun upon morning clouds that seem to be born just where they appear. Like a beam of light striking through some orifice, they shine upon Zacharias in the Temple. As the morning light finds the flowers, so found they the mother of Jesus. To the shepherds' eyes they filled the midnight arch like auroral beams of light; but not as silently, for they sang, and more marvellously than when "the morning stars sang together and all the sons of God shouted for joy."

The new era opens at Jerusalem. The pride with which a devout Jew looked upon Jerusalem can scarcely be imagined in our prosaic times.

Men loved that city with such passionate devotion as we are accustomed to see bestowed only on a living person. When the doctrine of immortality grew more distinctly into the belief of holy men, no name could be found which would make the invisible world so attractive as that of the beloved city. NEW JERUSALEM was the chosen name for Heaven.

Upon this city broke the morning rays of the Advent. A venerable priest, Zacharias, belonging to the retinue of the Temple, had spent his whole life in the quiet offices of religion. He was married, but childless. To him happened a surprising thing.

It was his turn to burn incense, — the most honorable function of the priestly office. Upon the great altar of sacrifice, outside the holy place, the burnt-offering was placed. At a signal the priest came forth, and, taking fire from this altar, he entered the inner and more sacred. place of the Temple, and there, before the altar of incense, putting the fragrant gum upon the coals, he swung the censer, filling the air with wreaths of smoke. The people who had gathered on the outside, as soon as the smoke ascended silently sent up their prayers, of which the incense was a symbol. "And there appeared unto him an angel of the Lord, standing on the right side of the altar."

That he trembled with fear and awe is apparent from the angel's address, — "Fear not!" The key-note of the new dispensation was sounded! Hereafter, God was to be brought nearer, to seem less terrible ; and a religion of the spirit and of love was soon to dispossess a religion of ceremonials and of fear.

> " Fear not, Zacharias : for thy prayer is heard ;
>   And thy wife Elisabeth shall bear thee a son,
>   And thou shalt call his name John.
>   And thou shalt have joy and gladness ;
>   And many shall rejoice at his birth.
>   For he shall be great in the sight of the Lord,
>   And shall drink neither wine nor strong drink ;
>   And he shall be filled with the Holy Ghost even from
>   his mother's womb.
>   And many of the children of Israel shall he turn to the
>   Lord their God.
>   And he shall go before him in the spirit and power of
>   Elias,
>   To turn the hearts of the parents to the children,
>   And the disobedient to the wisdom of the just ;
>   To make ready a people prepared for the Lord."

'If this address, to our modern ears, seems stately and formal, it is to be remembered that no other language would seem so fit for a heavenly message to a Jewish priest as that which breathed the spirit of the Old Testament writings; and that to us it savors of the sermon because it has since been so often used for the purposes of the sermon.

But the laws of the material world seemed to the doubting priest more powerful than the promise of that God who made all physical laws. To this distinct promise of a son who should become a great reformer, and renew the power and grandeur of the prophetic office, he could only say, "Whereby shall I know this?" His doubts should have begun earlier, or not at all. He should have rejected the whole vision, or should have accepted the promise implicitly ; for what sign could be given so assuring as the very presence of the angel? But the sign which he asked was given in a way that he could never forget. His speech departed : silence was the sign ; — as if the priest of the Old was to teach no more until the coming of the New.

When Zacharias came forth to the people, who

were already impatient at his long delay, they perceived by his altered manner that some great experience had befallen him. He could not speak, and could dismiss them only by a gesture.

We have no certainty whether this scene occurred at a morning or an evening service, but it is supposed to have been at the evening sacrifice. In that case the event was an impressive symbol. The people beheld their priest standing against the setting sun, dumb, while they dispersed in the twilight, the shadow of the Temple having already fallen upon them. The Old was passing into darkness; to-morrow another sun must rise!

Elisabeth, the wife of Zacharias, returned to the " hill-country," or that region lying west and south of Jerusalem. The promise had begun to be fulfilled. All the promises made to Israel were pointing to their fulfilment through her. These promises, accumulating through ages, were ample enough, even in the letter, to fill a devout soul with ardent expectancy. But, falling upon the imagination of a greatly distressed people, they had been magnified or refracted until the public mind was filled with inordinate and even fantastic expectations of the Messianic reign. It is not probable that any were altogether free from this delusion, not even the soberest and most spiritual natures. We can therefore imagine but faintly the ecstatic hopes of Zacharias and Elisabeth during the six months in which they were hidden in their home among the hills before the history again finds them. They are next introduced through the story of another memorable actor in this drama, the mother of our Lord.

It is difficult to speak of Mary, the mother of Jesus, both because so little is known of her and because so much has been imagined. Around no other name in history has the imagination thrown its witching light in so great a volume. In art she has divided honors with her divine Son. For a thousand years her name has excited the profoundest reverence and worship. A mother's love and forbearance with her children, as it is a universal experience, so is it the nearest image of the divine tenderness which the soul can form.

In attempting to present the Divine Being in his relations to universal government, men have well-nigh lost his personality in a sublime abstraction. Those traits of personal tenderness and generous love which alone will ever draw the human heart to God, it has too often been obliged to seek elsewhere. And, however mistaken the endeavor to find in the Virgin Mary the sympathy and fond familiarity of a divine fostering love, it is an error into which men have been drawn by the profoundest needs of the human soul. It is an error of the heart. The cure will be found by revealing, in the Divine nature, the longed-for traits in greater beauty and force than are given them in the legends of the mother of Jesus.

Meanwhile, if the doctors of theology have long hesitated to deify the Virgin, art has unconsciously raised her to the highest place. There is nothing in attitude, expression, or motion which has been left untried. The earlier Christian painters were content to express her pure fervor, without relying upon the element of beauty. But as, age by age, imagination kindled, the canvas has given forth this divine mother in more and more glowing beauty, borrowing from the Grecian spirit all that was charming in the highest ideals of Venus, and adding to them an element of transcendent purity and devotion which has no parallel in ancient art.

It is difficult for one whose eye has been steeped in the colors of art to go back from its enchantment to the barrenness of actual history. By Luke alone is the place even of her residence mentioned. It is only inferred that she was of the royal house of David. She was already espoused to a man named Joseph, but not as yet married. This is the sum of our knowledge of Mary at the point where her history is introduced. Legends abound, many of them charming ; but like the innumerable faces which artists have painted, they gratify the imagination without adding anything to historic truth.

The scene of the Annunciation will always be admirable in literature, even to those who are not disposed to accord it any historic value. To announce to an espoused virgin that she was to be the mother of a child, out of wedlock, by the unconscious working in her of the Divine power, would, beforehand, seem inconsistent with delicacy. But no person of poetic sensibility can read the scene as it is narrated by Luke without admiring its sublime purity and serenity. It is not a transaction of the lower world of passion. Things most difficult to a lower sphere are both easy and beautiful in that atmosphere which, as it were, the angel brought down with him.

"And the angel came in unto her and said, Hail! thou that art highly favored! The Lord is with thee!"

Then was announced the birth of Jesus, and that he should inherit and prolong endlessly the glories promised to Israel of old. To her inquiry, "How shall this be?" the angel replied: —

" The Holy Ghost shall come upon thee,
    And the power of the Highest shall overshadow thee;
    Therefore also that holy thing which shall be born of thee
    Shall be called the Son of God."

It was also made known to Mary that her cousin Elisabeth had conceived a son. And Mary said: "Behold the handmaid of the Lord! Be it unto me according to thy word."

Many have brought to this history the associations of a later day, of a different civilization, and of habits of thought foreign to the whole cast of the Oriental mind. Out of a process so unphilosophical they have evolved the most serious doubts and difficulties. But no one is fitted to appreciate either the beauty or the truthfulness to nature of such a scene, who cannot in some degree carry himself back in sympathy to that Jewish maiden's life. The education of a Hebrew woman was far freer than that of women of other Oriental nations. She had more personal liberty, a wider scope of intelligence, than obtained among the Greeks or even among the Romans. But above all, she received a moral education which placed her high above her sisters in other lands.

It is plain that Mary was imbued with the spirit of the Hebrew Scriptures. Not only was the history of her people familiar to her, but her language shows that the poetry of the Old Testament had filled her soul. She was fitted to receive her people's history in its most romantic and spiritual aspects. They were God's peculiar people. Their history unrolled before her as a series of wonderful providences. The path glowed with divine manifestations. Miracles blossomed out of every natural law. But to her there were no laws of nature. Such ideas had not yet been born. The earth was "the Lord's." All its phenomena were direct manifestations of his will. Clouds and storms came on errands from God. Light and darkness were the shining or the hiding of his face. Calamities were punishments. Harvests were divine gifts ; famines were immediate divine penalties. To us God acts through instruments; to the Hebrew he acted immediately by his will. " He spake, and it was done ; he commanded, and it stood fast."

To such a one as Mary there would be no incredulity as to the reality of this angelic manifestation. Her only surprise would be that *she* should be chosen for a renewal of those divine interpositions in behalf of her people of which their history was so full. The very reason which would lead us to suspect a miracle in our day gave it credibility in other days. It is simply a question of adaptation. A miracle as a blind appeal to the moral sense, without the use of the reason, was adapted to the earlier periods of human life. Its usefulness ceases when the moral sense is so developed that it can find its own way, through the ministration of the reason. A miracle is a substitute for moral demonstration, and is peculiarly adapted to the early conditions of mankind.

Of all miracles, there was none more sacred, congruous, and grateful to a Hebrew than an angelic visitation. A devout Jew, in looking back, saw angels flying thick between the heavenly throne and the throne of his fathers. The greatest events of national history had been made illustrious by their presence. Their work began with the primitive pair. They had come at evening to Abraham's tent. They had waited upon Jacob's footsteps. They had communed with Moses, with the judges, with priests and magistrates, with prophets and holy men. All the way down from the beginning of history, the pious Jew saw the shining footsteps of these heavenly messengers. Nor had the faith died out in the long interval through which their visits had been withheld. Mary could not, therefore, be surprised at the coming of angels, but only that they should come to her.

It may seem strange that Zacharias should be struck dumb for doubting the heavenly messenger, while Mary went unrebuked. But it is plain that there was a wide difference in the nature of the relative experiences. To Zacharias was promised an event external to himself, not involving his own sensibility. But to a woman's heart there can be no other announcement possible that shall so stir every feeling and sensibility of the soul, as the promise and prospect of her first child. Motherhood is the very centre of womanhood. The first

awaking in her soul of the reality that she bears a
double life — herself within herself — brings a
sweet bewilderment of wonder and joy. The
more sure her faith of the fact, the more tremulous
must her soul become. Such an announcement
can never mean to a father's what it does to a
mother's heart. And it is one of the exquisite
shades of subtle truth, and of beauty as well, that
the angel who rebuked Zacharias for doubt saw
nothing in the trembling hesitancy and wonder of
Mary inconsistent with a childlike faith.

If the heart swells with the hope of a new life in
the common lot of mortals, with what profound
feeling must Mary have pondered the angel's
promise to her son !

" He shall be great, and shall be called the Son of the
        Highest ;
.   And the Lord God shall give him the throne of his father
        David ;   .
    And he shall reign over the house of Jacob forever,
    And of his kingdom there shall be no end."

It is expressly stated that Joseph was of the
"house of David," but there is no evidence that
Mary was of the same, except this implication,

"The Lord God shall give him the throne of his father David." Since Joseph was not his father, it could only be through his mother that he could trace his lineage to David.

There is no reason to suppose that Mary was more enlightened than those among whom she dwelt, or that she gave to the angel's words that spiritual sense in which alone they have proved true. To her, it may be supposed, there arose a vague idea that her son was destined to be an eminent teacher and deliverer. She would naturally go back in her mind to the instances, in the history of her own nation, of eminent men and women who had been raised up in dark times to deliver their people.

She lived in the very region which Deborah and Barak had made famous. Almost before her eyes lay the plains on which great deliverances had been wrought by heroes raised up by the God of Israel. But that other glory, of spiritual deliverance, was hidden from her. Or, if the influence which overshadowed her awakened in her the spiritual vision, it was doubtless to reveal only that her son was to be something more than a mere worldly conqueror. But it was not for her to discern the glorious reality. It hung in the future as a dim brightness, whose particular form and substance could not be discerned. For it is not to be supposed that Mary — prophet as every woman is — could perceive that spiritual truth of the promises of the Old Testament which his own disciples did not understand after companying with Jesus for three years, nor yet after his ascension, nor until the fire of the pentecostal day had kindled in them the eye of flame that pierces all things and discerns the spirit.

"And Mary arose in those days and went into the hill-country with haste, into a city of Juda, and entered into the house of Zacharias and saluted Elisabeth."

The overshadowing Spirit had breathed upon her the new life. What woman of deep soul was ever unthrilled at the mystery of life beating within life? And what Jewish woman, devoutly believing that in her child were to be fulfilled the hopes of Israel, could hold this faith without excitement almost too great to be borne? She could not tarry. With haste she trod that way which she had doubtless often trod before in her annual ascent to the Temple. Every village, every

brook, every hill, must have awakened in her some
sad recollection of the olden days of her people.
There was Tabor, from which came down Barak
and his men. And in the great plain of Esdraelon he fought Sisera. The waters of Kishon, mur-
muring at her feet, must have recalled the song
of Deborah. Here, too, Josiah was slain at Me-
giddo, and "the mourning of Hadad-Rimmon in
the valley of Megiddon," became the byword of
grief. Mount Gilboa rose upon her from the east.
Ebal and Gerizim stood forth in remembrance
of the sublime drama of blessings and cursings.
Then came Shechem, the paradise of Palestine,
in whose neighborhood Joseph was buried. It
might be that the oak of Mamre, under which the
patriarch dwelt, cast its shadow on this pilgrim,
and she may have quenched her thirst at noonday,
as afterwards her son did, at the well of Jacob,
which was near by.

It is plain from the song of Mary, of which
we shall speak in a moment, that she bore in
mind the history of the mother of Samuel, wife
of Elkanah, who dwelt in this region, and
whose song, at the presentation of Samuel to
the priest at Shiloh, seems to have been the

mould in which Mary unconsciously cast her own.

Thus, one after another, Mary must have passed the most memorable spots in her people's history. Even if not sensitive to patriotic influences, — still more if she was alive to such sacred and poetic associations, — she must have come to her relative Elisabeth with flaming heart.

Well she might! What other mystery in human . life is so profound as the beginning of life? From the earliest days women have called themselves blessed of God when life begins to palpitate within their bosom. It is not education, but nature, that inspires such tender amazement. Doubtless even the Indian woman in such periods dwells consciously near to the Great Spirit! Every one of a deep nature seems to herself more sacred and more especially under the divine care while a new life, moulded by the divine hand, is springing into being. For, of all creative acts, none is so sovereign and divine. Who shall reveal the endless musings, the perpetual prophecies, of the mother's soul? Her thoughts dwell upon the unknown child, — thoughts more in number than the ripples of the sea upon some undiscovered shore. To

others, in such hours, woman should seem more
sacred than the most solemn temple; and to herself she must needs seem as if overshadowed by
the Holy Ghost.

To this natural elevation were added, in the in-
stance of Mary and Elisabeth, those vague but
exalted expectations arising from the angelic an-
nunciations. Both of them believed that the
whole future condition of their nation was to be
intimately affected by the lives of their sons.

And Mary said : —

"My soul doth magnify the Lord,
And my spirit hath rejoiced in God my Saviour.
For he hath regarded the low estate of his handmaiden ;
For, behold, from henceforth all generations shall call me
    blessed.
For He that is mighty hath done to me great things ;
And holy is his name.
And his mercy is on them that fear him
From generation to generation.
He hath shewed strength with his arm ;
He hath scattered the proud in the imagination of their
    hearts.
He hath put down the mighty from their seats,
And exalted them of low degree.
He hath filled the hungry with good things ;
And the rich he hath sent empty away.

He hath holpen his servant Israel,
In remembrance of his mercy ;
As he spake to our fathers,
To Abraham, and to his seed forever."

Unsympathizing critics remark upon the simi-
larity of this chant of Mary's with the song of
Hannah,* the mother of Samuel. Inspiration
served to kindle the materials already in pos-
session of the mind. This Hebrew maiden had

* " My heart rejoiceth in the Lord ;
   My horn is exalted in the Lord ;
   My mouth is enlarged over mine enemies ;
   Because I rejoice in thy salvation.
   There is none holy as the Lord ;
   For there is none beside thee ;
   Neither is there any rock like our God.
   Talk no more so exceeding proudly :
   Let not arrogancy come out of your mouth :
   For the Lord is a God of knowledge,
   And by him actions are weighed.
   The bows of the mighty men are broken,
   And they that stumbled are girded with strength.
   They that were full have hired out themselves for bread ;
   And they that were hungry ceased ;
   So that the barren hath borne seven ;
   And she that hath many children is waxed feeble.
   The Lord killeth, and maketh alive :
   He bringeth down to the grave, and bringeth up.

stored her imagination with the poetic elements of the Old Testament. But, of all the treasures at command, only a devout and grateful nature would have made so unselfish a selection. For it is not upon her own blessedness that Mary chiefly dwells, but upon the sovereignty, the goodness, and the glory of God. To be exalted by the joy of our personal prosperity above self-consciousness into the atmosphere of thanksgiving and adoration, is a sure sign of nobility of soul.

For three months these sweet and noble women

> The Lord maketh poor, and maketh rich :
> He bringeth low, and lifteth up.
> He raiseth up the poor out of the dust,
> And lifteth up the beggar from the dunghill,
> To set them among princes,
> And to make them inherit the throne of glory :
> For the pillars of the earth are the Lord's,
> And he hath set the world upon them.
> He will keep the feet of his saints,
> And the wicked shall be silent in darkness :
> For by strength shall no man prevail.
> The adversaries of the Lord shall be broken to pieces ;
> Out of heaven shall he thunder upon them :
> The Lord shall judge the ends of the earth ;
> And he shall give strength unto his King,
> And exalt the horn of his Anointed."

dwelt together, performing, doubtless, the simple labors of the household. Their thoughts, their converse, their employments, must be left wholly to the imagination. And yet it is impossible not to be curious in regard to these hidden days of Judæa, when the mother of our Lord was already fashioning that sacred form which, in due time, not far from her residence, perhaps within the very sight of it, was to be lifted up upon the cross. But it is a research which we have no means of pursuing. Her thoughts must be impossible to us, as our thoughts of her son were impossible to her. No one can look forward, even in the spirit of prophecy, to see after-things in all their fulness as they shall be; nor can one who has known go back again to see as if he had not known.

After Mary's return to Nazareth, Elisabeth was delivered of a son. Following the custom of their people, her friends would have named him after his father, but the mother, mindful of the name given by the angel, called him John. An appeal was made to the priest — who probably was deaf as well as dumb, for they made signs to him — how the child should be named. Calling for writing-materials, he surprised them all by naming him as his wife had, — John. At once the sign ceased. His lips were unsealed, and he broke forth into thanksgiving and praise. All the circumstances conspired to awaken wonder, and to spread throughout the neighborhood mysterious expectations, men saying, "What manner of child shall this be ? "

The first chapter of Luke may be considered as the last leaf of the Old Testament, so saturated is it with the heart and spirit of the olden times. And the song of Zacharias clearly reveals the state of feeling among the best Jews of that day. Their nation was grievously pressed down by foreign despotism. Their people were scattered through the world. The time was exceedingly dark, and the promises of the old prophets served by contrast to make their present distress yet darker. We are not surprised, therefore, to find the first portion of Zacharias's chant sensitively recognizing the degradations and sufferings of his people : —

" Blessed be the Lord God of Israel ;
  For he hath visited and redeemed his people,
  And hath raised up an horn of salvation for us

In the house of his servant David
(As he spake by the mouth of his holy prophets,
Which have been since the world began);
That we should be saved from our enemies,
And from the hand of all that hate us;
To perform the mercy promised to our fathers,
And to remember his holy covenant,
The oath which he sware to our father Abraham,
That he would grant unto us,
That we being delivered out of the hand of our enemies
Might serve him without fear,
In holiness and righteousness before him,
All the days of our life."

Then, as if seized with a spirit of prophecy, and beholding the relations and offices of his son, in language as poetically beautiful as it is spiritually triumphant he exclaims : —

" And thou, child, shalt be called the prophet of the Highest:
For thou shalt go before the face of the Lord to prepare
his ways;
To give knowledge of salvation unto his people
By the remission of their sins,
Through the tender mercy of our God;
Whereby the day-spring from on high hath visited us,
To give light to them that sit in darkness and in the
shadow of death,
To guide our feet into the way of peace."

Even in his childhood John manifested that fulness of nature and that earnestness which afterwards fitted him for his mission. He "waxed strong in spirit." He did not mingle in the ordinary pursuits of men. As one who bears a sensitive conscience and refuses to mingle in the throng of men of low morality, he stood apart and was solitary. He "was in the deserts until the day of his showing unto Israel."

Mary had returned to Nazareth. Although Joseph, to whom she was betrothed, was descended from David, every sign of royalty had died out. He earned his livelihood by working in wood, probably as a carpenter, though the word applied to his trade admits of much larger application. Tradition has uniformly represented him as a carpenter, and art has conformed to tradition. He appears but on the threshold of the history. He goes to Egypt, returns to Nazareth, and is faintly recognized as present when Jesus was twelve years of age. But nothing more is heard of him. If alive when his reputed son entered upon public ministry, there is no sign of it. And as Mary is often mentioned in the history of the Lord's mission, it is probable that Joseph died before Jesus entered upon his public life. He is called a just man, and we know that he was humane. For when he perceived the condition of his betrothed wife, instead of pressing to its full rigor the Jewish law against her, he meant quietly and without harm to set her aside. When in a vision he learned the truth, he took Mary as his wife.

In the thousand pictures of the Holy Family, Joseph is represented as a venerable man, standing a little apart, lost in contemplation, while Mary and Elisabeth caress the child Jesus. In this respect, Christian art has, it is probable, rightly represented the character of Joseph. He was but a shadow on the canvas. Such men are found in every community, — gentle, blameless, mildly active, but exerting no positive influence. Except in one or two vague implications, he early disappears from sight. No mention is made of his death, though he must have deceased long before Mary, who in all our Lord's ministry appears alone. He reappears in the ecclesiastical calendar as St. Joseph, simply because he was the husband of Mary, — a harmless saint, mild and silent.

An imperial order having issued for the taxing of the whole nation, it became necessary for every

one, according to the custom of the Jews, to re-
pair to the city where he belonged, for regis-
tration.*

From Nazareth to Bethlehem was about eighty
miles. Travelling slowly, as the condition of
Mary required, they would probably occupy about
four days in reaching their destination. Already
the place was crowded with others brought thither
on the same errand. They probably sought shelter in a cottage, for "the inn was full," and there
Mary gave birth to her child.

It is said by Luke that the child was laid in a
manger, from which it has been inferred that his
parents had taken refuge in a stable. But tradi-

---

* It is needless to consider the difficulty to which this passage
has given rise. Josephus states that Quirinius (Cyrenius) became
governor of Judæa after the death of Archelaus, Herod's son and
heir, and so some eight or ten years after the birth of Christ.
How then could that taxing have brought Joseph from Nazareth
to Bethlehem? The immense ingenuity which has been employed
to solve this difficulty will scarcely add to the value of hypothet-
ical historical reasoning. Especially when now, at length, it is
ascertained upon grounds almost certain, that Quirinius was *twice*
governor of Syria. See Schaff's note to Lange's *Com.* (Luke,
pp. 32, 33), and the more full discussion in Smith's *Bible Diction-
ary*, Art. "Cyrenius," and President Woolsey's addition to this
article in Hurd and Houghton's American edition.

tion asserts that it was a *cave*, such as abound in the limestone rock of that region, and are used both for sheltering herds and, sometimes, for human residences. The precipitous sides of the rock are often pierced in such a way that a cottage built near might easily convert an adjoining cave to the uses of an outbuilding.

Caves are not rare in Palestine, as with us. On the contrary, the whole land seems to be honey-combed with them. They are, and have been for ages, used for almost every purpose which architecture supplies in other lands, — as dwellings for the living and sepulchres for the dead, as shelter for the household and for cattle and herds, as hidden retreats for robbers, and as defensive positions or rock-castles for soldiers. Travellers make them a refuge when no better inn is at hand. They are shaped into reservoirs for water, or, if dry, they are employed as granaries. The limestone of the region is so porous and soft, that but little labor is required to enlarge, refashion, and adapt caves to any desirable purpose.

Of the "manger," or "crib," Thompson, long a missionary in Palestine, says : "It is common to find two sides of the one room, where the native farmer resides with his cattle, fitted up with these mangers, and the remainder elevated about two feet higher for the accommodation of the family. The mangers are built of small stones and mortar, in the shape of a box, or, rather, of a kneading-trough, and when cleaned up and whitewashed, as they often are in summer, they do very well to lay little babes in. Indeed, our own children have slept there in our rude summer retreats on the mountains." *

The laying of the little babe in the manger is not to be regarded then as an extraordinary thing, or a positive hardship. It was merely subjecting the child to a custom which peasants frequently practised with their children. Jesus began his life with and as the lowest.

About five miles south of Jerusalem, and crowning the top and sides of a narrow ridge or spur, which shoots out eastwardly from the central mass of the Judæan hills, was the village of Bethlehem. On every side but the western, the hill breaks down abruptly into deep valleys. The steep slopes were terraced and cultivated from top

* Thompson's *The Land and the Book*, Vol. II. p. 98.

to bottom. A little to the eastward is a kind of plain, where it is supposed the shepherds, of all shepherds that ever lived now the most famous, tended their flocks. The great fruitfulness of its fields is supposed to have given to Bethlehem its name, which signifies the "House of Bread." Famous as it has become, it was but a hamlet at the birth of Jesus. Here King David was born, but there is nothing to indicate that he retained any special attachment to the place. In the rugged valleys and gorges which abound on every side, he had watched his father's flocks and had become inured to danger and to toil, defending his charge on the one hand against wild beasts, and on the other against the scarcely less savage predatory tribes that infested the region south and east. From Bethlehem one may look out upon the very fields made beautiful forever to the imagination by the charming idyl of David's ancestress, Ruth the Moabitess. Changed as Bethlehem itself is, which, from holding a mere handful then, has a population now of some four thousand, customs and the face of nature remain the same. The hills are terraced, the fields are tilled, flocks are tended by laborers unchanged in garb, working with the same kinds of implements, having the same manners, and employing the same salutations as in the days of the patriarchs.

Were Boaz to return to-day, he would hardly see an unfamiliar thing in his old fields, — the barley harvest, the reapers, the gleaners, the threshing-floors, and the rude threshing, — all are there as they were thousands of years ago.

At the season of our Saviour's advent, the nights were soft and genial.* It was no hardship

---

* This is true, whichever date shall be selected of the many which have been urged by different learned men. But further than this there is no certainty. "In the primitive Church there was no agreement as to the time of Christ's birth. In the East the 6th of January was observed as the day of his baptism and birth. In the third century, as Clement of Alexandria relates, some regarded the 20th of May, others the 20th of April, as the birthday of our Saviour. Among modern chronologists and biographers of Jesus there is still greater difference of opinion, and every month — even June and July (when the fields are parched from want of rain) — has been named as the time when the great event took place. Lightfoot assigns the Nativity to September, Lardner and Newcome to October, Wieseler to February, Paulus to March, Greswell and Alfera to the 5th of April, just after the spring rains, when there is an abundance of pasture ; Lichtenstein places it in July or December, Strong in August, Robinson in autumn, Clinton in spring, Andrews between the middle of December, 749, and the middle of January, 750, A. U. C. On the

for rugged shepherds to spend the night in the
fields with their flocks. By day, as the sheep fed,
their keepers might while away their time with
sights and sounds along the earth. When darkness shut in the scene, the heavens would naturally attract their attention. Their eyes had
so long kept company with the mysterious stars,
that, doubtless, like shepherds of more ancient
times, they were rude astronomers, and had grown
familiar with the planets, and knew them in all
their courses. But there came to them a night
surpassing all nights in wonders. Of a sudden the
whole heavens were filled with light, as if morning
were come upon midnight. Out of this splendor a
single voice issued, as of a choral leader, — "Behold, I bring you glad tidings of great joy." The
shepherds were told of the Saviour's birth, and of
the place where the babe might be found. Then

other hand, Roman Catholic historians and biographers of Jesus,
as Lepp, Friedlieb, Bucher, Patritius, and also some Protestant
writers, defend the popular tradition, — the 25th of December.
Wordsworth gives up the problem, and thinks that the Holy
Spirit has concealed the knowledge of the year and day of
Christ's birth and the duration of his ministry from the wise and
prudent, to teach them humility." — Dr. Schaff, in Lange's *Com-
mentary* (Luke, p. 36).

no longer a single voice, but a host in heaven, was heard celebrating the event. "Suddenly there was with the angel a multitude of the heavenly host, praising God, and saying,

> " Glory to God in the highest,
> And on earth peace, good-will toward men."

Raised to a fervor of wonder, these children of the field made haste to find the babe, and to make known on every side the marvellous vision. Moved by this faith to worship and to glorify God, they were thus unconsciously the earliest disciples and the first evangelists, for " they made known abroad the saying which was told them concerning this child."

In beautiful contrast with these rude exclamatory worshippers, the mother is described as silent and thoughtful. " Mary kept all these things and pondered them in her heart." If no woman comes to herself until she loves, so, it may be said, she knows not how to love until her first-born is in her arms. Sad is it for her who does not feel herself made sacred by motherhood. That heart-pondering ! Who may tell the thoughts which rise

from the deep places of an inspired love, more in
number and more beautiful than the particles of
vapor which the sun draws from the surface of the
sea ?

Intimately as a mother must feel that her babe
is connected with her own body, even more she is
wont to feel that her child comes direct from God.
God-given is a familiar name in every language.
Not from her Lord came this child to Mary. It
was her Lord himself that came.

A sweet and trusting faith in God, childlike
simplicity, and profound love seem to have formed
the nature of Mary. She may be accepted as the
type of Christian motherhood. In this view, and
excluding the dogma of her immaculate nature,
and still more emphatically that of any other par-
ticipation in divinity than that which is common
to all, we may receive with pleasure the stores of
exquisite pictures with which Christian art has
filled its realm. The "Madonnas" are so many
tributes to the beauty and dignity of motherhood ; and they may stand so interpreted now
that the superstitious associations which they
have had are so wholly worn away. At any rate,
the Protestant reaction from Mary has gone far

enough, and on our own grounds we may well have our share also in the memory of this sweet and noble woman.

The same reason which led our Lord to clothe himself with flesh made it proper, when he was born, to have fulfilled upon him all the customs of his people. He was therefore circumcised when eight days old, and presented in the Temple on the fortieth day, at which period his mother had completed the time appointed for her purification. The offering required was a lamb and a dove ; but if the parents were poor, then two doves. Mary's humble condition was indicated by the offering of two doves. And yet, if she had heard the exclamation of John after the Lord's baptism, years afterwards, she might have perceived that, in spite of her poverty, she had brought the Lamb, divine and precious !

Surprise upon surprise awaited Mary. There dwelt at Jerusalem, wrapped in his own devout and longing thoughts, a great nature, living contentedly in obscurity, Simeon by name. This venerable man seized the child with holy rapture, when it was presented in the Temple, and broke forth in the very spirit of a prophet : —

" Lord, now lettest thou thy servant depart in peace,
   According to thy word :
   For mine eyes have seen thy salvation,
   Which thou hast prepared before the face of all people ;
   A light to lighten the Gentiles,
   And the glory of thy people Israel."

Both Mary and Joseph were amazed, but there was something in Mary's appearance that drew this inspired old man specially to her. " Behold, this child is set for the fall and rising again of many in Israel. . . . . Yea, a sword shall pierce through thine own soul also."

As the asters, among plants, go all summer long unbeautiful, their flowers hidden within, and burst into bloom at the very end of summer and in late autumn, with the frosts upon their heads, so this aged saint had blossomed, at the close of a long life, into this noble ecstasy of joy. In a stormy time, when outward life moves wholly against one's wishes, he is truly great whose soul becomes a sanctuary in which patience dwells with hope. In one hour Simeon received full satisfaction for the yearnings of many years !

Among the Jews, more perhaps than in any other Oriental nation, woman was permitted to develop naturally, and liberty was accorded her to participate in things which other people reserved with zealous seclusion for men. Hebrew women were prophetesses, teachers (2 Kings xxii. 14), judges, queens. The advent of our Saviour was hailed appropriately by woman, — Anna, the prophetess, joining with Simeon in praise and thanksgiving.

But other witnesses were preparing. Already the footsteps of strangers afar off were advancing toward Judæa. Erelong Jerusalem was thrown into an excitement by the arrival of certain sages, probably from Persia. The city, like an uneasy volcano, was always on the eve of an eruption. When it was known that these pilgrims had come to inquire about a king, who, they believed, had been born, a king of the Jews, the news excited both the city and the palace, — hope in one, fear in the other. Herod dreaded a rival. The Jews longed for a native prince whose arm should expel the intrusive government. No wonder that " Herod was troubled, and all Jerusalem with him." He first summoned the Jewish scholars, to know where, according to their prophets, the Messiah was to be born. Bethlehem was the place of prediction. Next, he summoned the Magi, secretly, to learn of them at what time the revealing star had appeared to them, and then, craftily veiling his cruel purposes with an assumed interest, he charges them, when the child was found, to let him be a worshipper too!

The same star which had drawn their footsteps to Jerusalem now guided the wise men to the very place of Jesus' birth.

What was this star? All that can be known is, that it was some appearance of light in the sky, which by these Oriental philosophers was supposed to indicate a great event. Ingenuity has unnecessarily been exercised to prove that at about this time there was a conjunction of three planets. But did the same thing happen again after their arrival at Jerusalem? For it is stated that on their leaving the city to go to Bethlehem, "lo, the star which they saw in the east went before them till it came and stood over where the young child was." How could a planetary conjunction stand over a particular house? It is evident that the sidereal guide was a globe of light divinely ordered and appointed for this work. It was a miracle. That nature is but an organized outworking of the divine will, that God is not limited to ordinary law in the production of results, that he can, and that he does, produce events by the direct force of his will without the ordinary instruments of nature, is the very spirit of the whole Bible.

These gleams of immediate power flash through in every age. The superiority of spiritual power over sensuous is the illuminating truth of the New Testament. The gospels should be taken or rejected unmutilated. The disciples plucked the wheat-heads, and, rubbing them in their hands, they ate the grain. But our sceptical believers take from the New Testament its supernatural element, — rub out the wheat, — and eat the chaff. There is consistency in one who sets the gospels aside on the ground that they are not inspired, that they are not even historical, that they are growths of the imagination, and covered all over with the parasites of superstition ; but in one who professes to accept the record as an inspired history, the disposition to pare miracles down to a scientific shape, to find their roots in natural laws, is neither reverent nor sagacious. Miracles are to be accepted boldly or not at all. They are jewels, and sparkle with divine light, or they are nothing.

This guide of the Magi was a light kindled in the heavens to instruct and lead those whose eyes were prepared to receive it. If the vision of angels and the extraordinary conception of the Virgin are received as miraculous, it ought not to be difficult to accept the star in the east as a miracle also.

The situation of the child ill befitted Oriental notions of a king's dignity. But under the divine influence which rested upon the Magi, they doubtless saw more than the outward circumstances. Humble as the place was, poor as his parents evidently were, and he a mere babe, they fell down before him in worship, and presented princely gifts, "gold, frankincense, and myrrh." Instead of returning to Herod, they went back to their own country.

And now it was time for Joseph to look well to his safety. If there was to be a king in Israel, he was to come from the house of David, and Joseph was of that stock, and his child, Jesus, was royal too. Herod's jealousy was aroused. He was not a man wont to miss the fulfilment of any desire on account of humane or moral scruples. The return of the Magi without giving him the knowledge which he sought seemed doubtless to the king like another step in a plot to subvert his throne. He determined to make thorough work of this nascent peril, "and sent forth and slew all the children that were in Bethlehem, and in all the coasts thereof, from two years old and under." He put the limit of age at a period which would make it sure that the new-born king of the Jews would be included.

It has been objected to the probable truth of this statement, that such an event could hardly fail to be recorded by secular historians, and especially by Josephus, who narrates the contemporaneous history with much minuteness. But this event is far more striking upon our imagination now, than it was likely to be upon the attention of men then. For, as Bethlehem was a mere hamlet, with but a handful of people, it has been computed that not more than ten or fifteen children could have perished by this merciless edict. Besides, what was such an act as this, in a life stored full of abominable cruelties? "He who had immolated a cherished wife, a brother, and three sons to his jealous suspicions, and who ordered a general massacre for the day of his funeral, so that his body

should not be borne to the earth amidst general
rejoicings," may easily be supposed to have filled
up the spaces with minor cruelties which escaped
record. But here *is* an historical record. It is no
impeachment of its truth to aver that there is no
other history of it. Until some disproof is alleged,
it must stand.

Stirred by a divine impulse, Joseph had already
removed the child from danger. Whither should
he flee ? Egypt was not distant, and the roads
thither were easy and much frequented. Thither
too, from time to time, exiled for various reasons,
had resorted numbers of Jews, so that, though in
a foreign land, he would be among his own
countrymen, all interested alike in hating the
despotic cruelty of Herod. There is no record of
the place of Joseph's sojourn in Egypt. Tradition, always uncertain, places it at Matarea, near
Leontopolis, where subsequently the Jewish temple
of Onias stood.

His stay was probably brief. For, within two
or three weeks of the foregoing events, Herod
died. Joseph did not return to Bethlehem, though
he desired to do so, but was warned of God in a
dream of his danger. It was probable that Arche-

laus, who succeeded to Herod in Judæa, would be as suspicious of danger from an heir royal of the house of David as his father had been; so Joseph passed — it may be by way of the sea-coast — northward, to Nazareth, whence a few months before he had removed.

Before closing, we shall revert to one of the most striking features of the period thus far passed over, namely, *the ministration of angels.* The belief in the existence of heavenly beings who in some manner are concerned in the affairs of men, has existed from the earliest periods of which we have a history. This faith is peculiarly grateful to the human heart, and, though it has never been received with favor by men addicted to purely physical studies, it has been entertained by the Church with fond faith and by the common people with the enthusiasm of sympathy.

It is scarcely possible to follow the line of development in the animal kingdom, and to witness its gradations on the ascending scale, unfolding steadily, rank above rank, until man is reached, without having the presumption awakened that there are intelligences above man, — creatures which rise as much above him as he above the inferior animals.

When the word of God announces the ministration of angels, records their early visits to this planet, represents them as bending over the race in benevolent sympathy, bearing warnings, consolations, and messages of wisdom, the heart receives the doctrine even against the cautions of a sceptical reason.

Our faith might be put to shame if the scriptural angels bore any analogy to those of the rude and puerile histories contained in apocryphal books. But the long line of heavenly visitants shines in unsullied brightness as high above the beliefs and prejudices of an early age as the stars are above the vapors and dust of earth. While patriarchs, prophets, and apostles show all the deficiencies of their own period and are stained with human passions, the angelic beings, judged by the most fastidious requirements of these later ages, are without spot or blemish. They are not made up of human traits idealized. They are unworldly, — of a different type, of nobler presence, and of far grander and sweeter natures than any living on earth. The angels of the oldest records are like the angels of the latest. The Hebrew thought had moved through a vast arc of the infinite cycle of truth between the days when Abraham came from Ur of Chaldæa and the times of our Lord's stay on earth. But there is no development in angels of later over those of an earlier date. They were as beautiful, as spiritual, as pure and noble, at the beginning as at the close of the old dispensation. Can such creatures, transcending earthly experience, and far outrunning anything in the life of man, be creations of the rude ages of the human understanding?

We could not imagine the Advent stripped of its angelic lore. The dawn without a twilight, the

sun without clouds of silver and gold, the morning
on the fields without dew-diamonds, — but not the
Saviour without his angels! They shine within
the Temple, they bear to the matchless mother a
message which would have been disgrace from
mortal lips, but which from theirs fell upon her as
pure as dew-drops upon the lilies of the plain of
Esdraelon. They communed with the Saviour in
his glory of transfiguration, sustained him in the
anguish of the garden, watched at the tomb ; and
as they had thronged the earth at his coming,
so they seem to have hovered in the air in mul-
titudes at the hour of his ascension. Beautiful as
they seem, they are never mere poetic adornments.
The occasions of their appearing are grand. The
reasons are weighty. Their demeanor suggests
and befits the highest conception of superior beings. These are the very elements that a rude age
could not fashion. Could a sensuous age invent an
order of beings which, touching the earth from a
heavenly height on its most momentous occasions,
could still, after ages of culture had refined the
human taste and moral appreciation, remain ineffa-
bly superior in delicacy, in pure spirituality, to the
demands of criticism ? Their very coming and

going is not with earthly movement. They suddenly are seen in the air as one sees white clouds
round out from the blue sky, in a summer's day,
that melt back even while one looks upon them.
They vibrate between the visible and the invisible.
They come without motion. They go without
flight. They dawn and disappear. Their words
are few, but the Advent Chorus yet is sounding
its music through the world.

A part of the angelic ministration is to be
looked for in what men are by it incited to do.
It helps the mind to populate heaven with spiritual inhabitants. The imagination no longer trans-
lates thither the gross corporeity of this life. We
suspect that few of us are aware how much our
definite conceptions of spirit-life are the product
of the angel-lore of the Bible.

It is to be noticed that only in Luke is the
history of the angelic annunciation given. It is to
Luke also that we are indebted for the record of
the angels at the tomb on the morning of the res-
urrection. Luke has been called the Evangelist
of Greece. He was Paul's companion of travel,
and particularly among the Greek cities of Asia
Minor. This suggests the fact that the angelic

ministration commemorated in the New Testament
would greatly facilitate among Greeks the recep-
tion of monotheism. Comforting to us as is the
doctrine of angels, it can hardly be of the same
help as it was to a Greek or to a Roman when he
first accepted the Christian faith. The rejection
of so many divinities must have left the fields, the
mountains, the cities and temples, very bare to all
who had been accustomed to heathen mythology.
The ancients seem to have striven to express universal divine presence by multiplying their gods.
This at least had the effect of giving life to every
part of nature. The imaginative Greek had grown
familiar with the thought of gods innumerable.
Every stream, each grove, the caves, the fields, the
clouds, suggested some divine person. It would
be almost impossible to strip such a one of those
fertile suggestions and tie him to the simple doctrine of One God, without producing a sense of
cheerlessness and solitude. Angels come in to
make for him an easy transition from polytheism
to monotheism. The air might still be populous,
his imagination yet be full of teeming suggestions,
but no longer with false gods. Now there was to
him but one God, but He was served by multi-

tudes of blessed spirits, children of light and glory. Instead of a realm of conflicting divinities there was a household, the Father looking in benignity upon his radiant family. Thus, again, to the Greek, as to the Patriarch, angels ascended and descended the steps that lead from earth to heaven.